BETA 2020

DEEPAK GUPTA

No.8, 3rd Cross Street,CIT Colony,
Mylapore, Chennai, Tamil Nadu-600004

ISBN 978-1-64805-289-7

Contents

Contents

Also By Deepak Gupta

The Girl with No Dreams 2019
5 Principles to Dig Out Success 2019
Powerful Quotes 2019
She's the Sunflower 2019
The Men who Forgets 2019
Revenge 2019
The Power of Universe 2019
Average Mind 2019
10 Principles to Love Yourself 2019
The Power of Nothing 2018
10 Principles to Beat Failure 2018
The Lost Child 2018
Zero Degree 2018
Wild Wife 2018
Skyfall 2018
Earth 2200 2018
Broken with Love 2018
Lionel Messi 2017
Time Management 2017
The Haunted Bridge 2017
She 2017
Top Business Secrets 2017
The Universe of your Mind 2017
One Rupee Business Law 2016
The Exorcism of Emily Rose 2016
Revolutionary Love 2016
Real Horror Stories 2016
Inspiring Life 2015

Prologue

Everyone wants to be happy all the time but life changes when we run behind happiness all the time and still feel anxiety and agony inside our mind and heart. **Why this is happening with all of us**is really a strange bad thought we face every day. We try to get happy and do any life activity to divert our minds with people, relatives, and friends and sometimes even with strangers. It's not much strange as the people around us also feel the same as we feel all the time. *We are chasing happiness forgot that happiness can never be chased* and anyone can find it inside even when the person is all alone. We taught it wrong to be with people or with our life partner for our happiness and peace. **Happiness is a very personal feeling and anyone can find it alone.**Until we find why and where happiness is missing, we would run behind it all our life.

I meet a lot of people every day who are not happy even after achieving a lot in life. They have everything except peace. **Where is peace in our life?**We spend time with friends, wander places and when we come to our home, we find ourselves lonely because no one teaches us how to be alone when we face such situations in life. How to control our thoughts when we are alone? Everyone is getting married because people usually say what we would do alone with our life. More stress in life; more will be the depression and ruined life. We don't have to fear when we actually face fear. We should learn the value of fear at the right time and move on in life. Beta 2020 is the book I always wanted to write but I was not enough good to write it in a better way. *Once we understand why we are unhappy, happiness will surround us for sure.*I was also unhappy for what I don't have but realised once I prayed for the present time in my past and enlightenment starts to begin in my life. I will make the book precise and effective to make it vital and productive for your time. ***Welcome to the Beta 2020 where only you can respond to your life; where only you can give feedback to your life and once it would happen, life would surely start to change in the right direction.***

CHAPTER ONE

Hate People Once

Hate people once to know whether they really love you or trading love with your love. I meet people regularly both online and personally, don't judge anyone. People are really good and sometimes strange. We don't judge anyone. ***People may hate us back for a short period of time but if they really love us they wouldn't leave us even in any situation of life.***If people leave us without resolving the conflicts then we are maintaining relationships for their happiness and to fulfil their togetherness in the lonely World.

The above principle can help us to remove toxic people from our life, at least the people who don't love us, anyway. Not everyone loves us as they show us in real life. People are different to expect love and give nothing in return. Before expecting anything we should learn to give.

Moreover, People are strange but we can understand them after a reasonable period of time. Meet people, understand them and love unconditionally are the best ways to enrich life with peace. Get attached to the people who have the calibre to accept our good habits and scars as well. Not the year 2020 but every year we need to hear and learn that true people are significant in life whether we are with one person or one million. No matter.

Every person we allow in our life; should be a person who talks with happiness, not with the daily chaos. Surround the right vibes and feel the beautiful changes in life. Don't cut with the people who are honest with their trouble. Do your best to help them. It's your call to observe and see, who is honest and who is not.

CHAPTER TWO

Happiness Without Cause

Have we ever thought about our happiness without cause? Now a day everything comes with a cause. Have we ever seen people's happiness without cause? Of course tough to answer but certain people are happy without a cause.

People find people to create happiness in life, that's the biggest lie we have ever applied and believed. *If happiness comes with a cause, it would go away with that cause.* Be happy and energetic whether you are alone or with someone else. Now a day people want to be with the person who is always happy because they find ways to reduce stress in life. They also have a cause to live happily. We don't need people to live happiness. We need a mind which can see big happiness in small activities of life. People become unhappy when they grow up. They find the little activities boring that brought us happiness in the past. Children are happy because they have the curiosity to see and feel everything. They find the environment interesting & that's why they look cheerful always. Happiness is always around us. Don't we feel happy when we see the butterfly? Then why are we unhappy! Do anything but with a happy face and we would get more than what we actually do.

'Happiness doesn't need a cause but needs a mind & heart that can believe happiness in small activities of life.'

Loneliness + Happiness = A right person who can manage any situations in life.

People + People = More happiness but more dependence in life.

BETA 2020
DEEPAK GUPTA

The above equations are most significant. Make a better trade-off to find the right people with the right happiness.

DEEPAK GUPTA

Change for Yourself, Not for Others

If someone hates us and we hate back in return then we change for others, not for ourselves. The best way to save energy is to sit calm and don't respond to those who don't believe in our ideas and hate us without any cause. *Hate without cause is drastic.* Sometimes we change for wrong, not for the right and that occupies space in our mind for long. Our mind works well when we utilise our brain cells in the same direction. Confusion creates nothing.

Most people change after seeing the behaviour of other people and that's too wrong. If we see our other side in the mirror doesn't mean we are the mirror or we are in the mirror. We create what we expect. The real one is inside us. Change is good until it doesn't change what we actually are. We need the change because we feel it from inside, not from the reflection of other people we meet and see every day. Every happy and sad person affects us positively and negatively. Both may be drastic in the long run. Meet people but don't change for anyone. If someone hates us then the best response is no response to free our mind from any tumult.

We don't need to get the colour of the people on our skin. Our skin and mind have own creation and we need to appreciate it without getting effect with anyone's mind and intentions.

Care and appreciate your mind and change is necessary. Do it for yourself, not for others.

CHAPTER FOUR

Manage Thoughts When You're Alone (Must Apply)

Thoughts are powerful when it comes to make and destroy human peace and life. ***If we can control our thoughts, we can do anything.*** We can achieve any tasks we want in life. Our thoughts help us in taking effective decisions but when it gets out of control, we make the decisions that we never think of. We manage our thoughts with others because everyone has an effect on our mind that's why I always recommend you to choose the people wisely. We don't know what we do when we are alone with our thoughts. Most of the difficult task in life is to manage thoughts when we are alone and when we are with ourselves in a room. Now the question is; How to think well to make anything predictable and achievable? Sometimes I also find difficult to manage thoughts as I am always flooded with ideas, innovation, and unwanted thoughts. Our brain first perceives the activities we do daily. Activities we do everything strikes in our mind first. It depends on how strong we are to think in the right direction to take the right decisions.

We think what we see and observe what we perceive the whole day, weeks and years.*Forgetting is almost impossible, better is to control it for a lifetime.*Our mind has also the backup plan, once we think about the past; it picks the thread to reach everywhere. We connect the dots of events and sometimes it makes us happy and sometimes a bit frustrated when the unwanted thoughts get surround us even when we don't want to and we over think in between. Not every time the thoughts are bad. *In my opinion, thoughts are the treasure of plans, ideas, innovation, and history.* We should know and understand how to manage our thoughts when we are alone.

To avoid over-thinking; people do unproductive tasks or to make unnecessary useless work to get busy. This doesn't change anything. Unnecessary thoughts will come back when we would finish the work. Nothing will change for permanent. The difficult situation is; we can't avoid the situation of over-thinking. The best way to stop it is to think about why we are over-thinking. Why are we getting such thoughts? *Give the right direction to your thoughts, convert it into goals and make your thoughts productive.*Sometimes I am also the one who over thinks and wakes up in the middle of the night. It's the fight we do within ourselves and people don't know about it. It takes away peace. Talk to yourself. When we start to talk to ourselves, we start to understand. Both are different. Think about is this you really deserve in life. Who are you and why are you? Do the activities you love the most. Don't try to be happy while over-thinking. It doesn't solve anything. Just stop that makes you close to the stress and depression of thoughts.

We are surrounded by people. More people bring more stories in our minds & in the age of competition, even in the corner, everyone wants to achieve better than others.

These types of situations also hamper our minds. Think but don't over-think and after some time you would feel better for achieve anything in life. ***The direction is significant. Just stop & start making & grow under the activities you love.***

CHAPTER FIVE

Productivity and Procrastination (2P'S)

'Some people think in the bathroom while some don't even work at the workplace. Being busy is not always productive.'

We know people are different so that's the biggest opportunity to learn from the differences in people. Every person has different attributes to respond to situations in life. Learn Productivity from the people in silence. *People we meet are actually the opportunities to learn from them, to teach them how different individuals have differences.*Some may be beautiful or weird. No matter. The matter is what we can bring out; that improves our life.

According to my opinion, productivity has nothing to do with time.

People procrastinate for two reasons:

1. First, they haven't achieved their planned tasks in life.
2. Second, are the ones who think they've achieved everything in life.

Both the above situations are drastic in life. *Over-commitment and undervaluation both are dangerous and lead to Procrastination in life.*People are lazy because self-inspiration is missing and they think they have nothing to do with the people and life. People are living life around own life but sometimes it hampers our creativity. The more unwanted and unproductive thoughts wander in our minds, we would mess anything even the planned ones. Think till its required and we can implement any lesson in our life.

CHAPTER SIX

How to do Self-Love When we are Broken Heart

When we love someone we should understand self love before it. Most of the people are heartbroken these days because they break their hearts for the wrong people. When we love someone so deeply, we get attached to that person. *Our attraction, affection, and love become our obsession sometimes*and we find our life difficult to continue without that person but it happens when we rush to possess person in our life. *Fear to lose someone brings more fear in our minds.*The true one will never leave without any tough reason. Everyone does mistakes and sometimes we also leave. We suffer and life becomes a miserable situation.

If we love someone deeply and unconditionally, let them go because that's true love. Freedom is the first rule to love someone and love ourselves. We can love but can't possess someone for our love. Love is the feeling which can be smelled through distances, can be understood through miles. In love one-sided lovers underestimate themselves because they think the person he/she loves will surely love back after a time but it doesn't happen most of the time. Self-love is much significant these days. *If we can't find our happiness and love when we are alone then we would always be lonely even with the crowd.*Self- love helps us to find out what we really like, what we see and true people will come because if someone loves us for reason then it wouldn't continue for long. *Self-made love can't be broken. It revives anything, almost everything.*

CHAPTER SEVEN

Obsession in Friendship

Some days when we are friends then we call it our friendship but if it becomes an obsession then it's no longer the friendship. *Obsession in Friendship is a dangerous turn in friendship.*

*The moment we live alone, look extraordinary when we live it with our best friends.*Best friends teach us to live life but when it becomes an obsession, it would ruin the friendship. In this chapter, I will tell you how to continue and hold friendship for a longer period of time. We make memories with friends and we don't forget it. Situation changes when it starts to surround our personal life. Whenever we wake or sleep, the moments chase us. I'm not saying the friendship is not good to go but obsession can be deadly.

Best friends are lifeline for a reason because they teach us to live moments carelessly in our real selves. They are lifeline in every century. We listen to many stories from our friends. Life teases us when we come back home after meeting with our friends. When we find happiness we can't leave the situations alone. We want to be with our best friends so that we don't have to be lonely, that's an obsession with friendship.

Live with best friends and be happy but also the same happiness should grow within ourselves when we are alone. The outer happiness should be equal to inner happiness.

The above equation makes sense in friendship and you will always find yourself cheerful and enthusiastic.

I hope people are happy as they look in photos and with friends.

CHAPTER EIGHT

Children's Attitude: Little Moments are Really Big Moments

A child is always happy because he's always curious about his environment. He sees small moments as big moments and treats it the same, may be innocently but that's our true image when we born. We get attached to the people, affect and our process starts to change. *A child has a better attitude than an adult one.*Curiosity is the real home of our soul. When we don't care about people, we are real. Present yourself and feel every moment.

*In 21st-century people think about accumulating wealth and resources & plan to enjoy later, that's the wrong attitude in life.*A child enjoys what he has and sometimes gets stubborn but never ruin happiness for it. The moment is going, life is going. We can't tell anyone to live later. Little moments are big moments in life when we are growing in our life. Never forget the power of weirdness within us. Laugh as hard you can. When we grow up, the moments we were really enjoying, look like small moments and we start to chase something else and happiness vanished in between.

Remember childhood is not an age, it's an attitude. There's a child in every human we meet. It will come out if we do the same for it. Realise it before it's too late. Wealth is the sign of security, a better standard of living and richness but happiness is really a different attribute. Grow the child inside you with the daily environment to feel light, cool and stress-free life. Have fun, laugh hard and remember goals, be serious but don't ruin your happiness for it.

First, we moved toward the city then we start to remember rural areas, knowing that we are the ones who are destroying the urban areas.

CHAPTER NINE

Half Way or No Way

Half way or no way chapter affects most of the young adults in the world. People are stressed because they want attention in life. ***People want to get encouraged and feel privileged when they come in surrounding with anyone.***When we don't get such appreciation, the stress begins in our life. Recognition in life is significant but not as bad as we want. We meet many people in our life but a few come and stay in our lives for a longer period. Love the people who stay the long way than the people who leave in between the half way. In the 21st century, we live with expectations, why? Why we need recognition for our presence.

I find the people better who don't come in our life or stay like a normal person who talks casually than the people who live half way in our life. Stop expecting love. ***Love grows when we stop responding to the wrong people in our life.*** To get recognition, stop being liked by the people. Do what you can do for long and be happy. Stop being a fool to be in the wrong people's life. Sometimes we leave the people still think about them; that's the worst situation. Change it. Stop being forcing but don't leave the right people in life.

Always have the habit if we leave wrong people, remove it from the mind as well then we will totally be unattached and can focus on life ahead.

Wake Up Tired? Why?

The biggest challenge in life is to wake up with an honest smile & happiness in our heart even when we have million dollars in our pocket. People have a millions of dollars but why are they not happy? It really matters. Stress and happiness both are everywhere. Both are easy and difficult at the same time. We sleep 8 hours a day, still feel tired? Why? Because our body sleeps but the mind still awake all the time even while sleeping. To calm our minds with all the chaos should be our first priority. Have some time to think nothing and have rest. Whatever we do, we do for happiness and peace and to prevent problems in life then why we are running behind stress to achieve heights in life.

Calm your mind before you sleep. Wake and don't rush for work initially. Spend time, do your favourite activities. Wake up with happiness & you would feel more sense of accomplishment than others & feel extra zest to achieve goals in a proper and better way.

'Stress kills our productivity every day. It kills us every second. Our challenge is to find ways & give direction to our mind to wake up happy, energetic and with positive vibes to achieve our dreams.

CHAPTER ELEVEN

How to Work in the Comfort Zone

Most people say if we want to achieve success in life then we have to come out from our comfort zone. I want to correct something in it. If we always try to achieve the tasks that don't belong to us then we always have to come out from our comfort zone. In all my books, I always say, do what you love because life is short enough and do what brings peace to your mind with the comfort zone. Go beyond the limit but don't push where you don't belong yourself. ***Change is essential but complete change is drastic.***Everyone is born with something, some attributes and it would change our life if we try to look inside. We would realise life starts to change, not this year but in whole life.

Now how to work in the comfort zone?The Comfort zone is the space where we can push our limits without changing ourselves. People love us for some reasons but if we get change to achieve our goals then it would get drastic in the long run.

We can achieve the best in which we are productive and Productivity comes with the environment we always want to work.

CHAPTER TWELVE

How to Prefer Passion Over Money

People are in dilemma these days about whether to follow passion or early money in life. Both are necessary for real life but we are fascinated by what we get early in life than to think of what can give benefit in the long run. *What can give happiness in the long run? We have to choose whether we should work for money or to work for happiness. Both are really different.*Money is an important part of our life because without it we can't survive but sometimes with it, people die with stress. **Go for money but don't forget to do what brings happiness on our face.**

After a few years, we would realise that we could prefer our passion over money. Passion brings happiness at present than to leave happiness on the money with great uncertainty. Money also brings happiness but it depends on how we utilise it in our life. It doesn't matter with the figures of your bank balance. *Money should be secondary when it becomes primary.*When I started to write books in 2015, I got nothing for the first three years and yes I was much disappointed because passion can't fill our empty stomach. I was disappointed but not sad in my life. I was tired but not stressed. I was writing books because it was my passion to have some peace and happiness in my life. I didn't start writing for money. We can't deny money in our life but it's not always the primary luxury we are searching for.

Work for happiness, not for money. Work for peace, not to get busy with it.

CHAPTER THIRTEEN

Unhappy Adults

We are broken with higher expectations and low responsiveness.

We were the happy children who used to enjoy even our ice-creams but as we grow up, we forget what happiness was for us. We become unhappy adults, how and why? What we think for others, we grow it inside. If we think better for others, we would become best. Our mind occupies us better and sometimes it becomes difficult to control it. If we want to be happy, do well for others. Don't keep anything negative inside your mind. What we think we become in reality. Respond to the right ones is fine. Don't hurt the right ones because of the wrong ones. Make a path of clear and understandable thoughts in your mind. Don't fight inside the mind. Remember the good what people do for us. People also do bad for us and everyone does but focuses on how they are good. *Unhappy adults are less productive and more aggressive. You will always find them aggressive and in frustration.*They don't talk to you properly and always in hurry to achieve tasks in life. Unhappy adults hide behind the occasional events where they can get happy and forget their real stress. They hide sometimes among the friend's happiness and find ways to become glad instead to know why they are unhappy.

Why our parents were happy in their time because they were surrounded by fewer people. The more people we surround ourselves, the more happiness & sadness would bring when they start to fade away from our life. This doesn't mean we shouldn't get surround by more people but get surround by right and true people are essential and these types of people are really less in life.

I always talk and write about the primary and basic principles of life because we overlook the simple things in life which ultimately would become difficult situations in our life. ***Remember happiness is easy for children and tough for adults because we are in hurry to understand the difficult things than to understand the simple things in life.***

CHAPTER FOURTEEN

How to Choose Love and Friendship

Most of the people initially falling in friendship than after fall in love but that's not always true in most of the cases. Love and friendship both are really different when we start to understand both in the 21st century.

When we spend time with anyone we feel like we are in love with them but that doesn't mean it is actually. Love is a different relationship from friendship. In friendship we laugh hard, do weird activities, eat together and think deeply but there's one attribute missing that love really takes care of, to leave hands even in any situation over the whole life. Some days friends also leave us and we also do the same. ***Friendship can be for a long time but rarely for a life time.*** When we love someone we accept their scars first and beauty later because we shouldn't find any reason to leave them in the future. Love accepts every attribute but somewhere whether we feel or not, it has the cause, any cause but that doesn't mean the friendship is bad. I'm trying to make a decision about how to choose Love and friendship in the 21st century. Don't test people in life and the wrong ones would automatically go out of your life.

In friendship, we laugh & leave hands in tears at some point in life.

In love, we laugh and hold hands for a lifetime.

Getting broken in love is not bad but hates someone after love is worst. Don't do it to anyone. Don't hurt anyone just because they don't love us. Everyone has the right to take life decisions, don't you take the decisions to love someone! Being broken but honest in your love.

Choose love wisely in life. Love can make anything & ruin as well.

There may be love in friendship but there should always friendship in love.

CHAPTER FIFTEEN

How to overcome Depression, Anxiety, Stress & a hopeless life (Animal Theory)

It's not strange when we come to know that we are the only reason for our depression and anxiety in our life. We do it ourselves by creating unnecessary thoughts in our minds.

We grow depression with our thoughts, once we come to know, we are strong, and no one can bring stress on our face.

Likewise, if happiness is an inner feeling, stress & depression are also growing within us. We grow both in our mind. Blaming everyone for our agony makes us mad and after we would attract more anxiety. I'm suggesting you to do the activity which I do every day. Most of the stress comes when we have pending tasks and we procrastinate every day. Procrastination makes our mind to think later and tired right now. We plan much better and get tired. Every day when you wake up in the morning, don't think about failure or any pending tasks for one hour. Just focus on what you want to do and what you love. Relax and calm your mind otherwise, the mind would get tired in the morning. After doing this activity, we would be more productive for the whole day. A ***tired mind is deadly than a tired body. If your body sleeps, you should ensure your mind should be.***

Failure in life is better than procrastination because in procrastination we do nothing, which means null productivity. To reduce stress from life, I have made an animal theory that can help us to think better.

Animal Theory: Animals are innocent because they don't use their mind for extra activities in life rather than to eat, sleep and breed. Of course, they love their master but don't think above it. Every human who cares for them, become their master. Simple as that. Animals are happy for fewer things. When we born we also born with animal attributes and we start to gain and absorb education and values from our environment and also from the people around us. Those who care and feed us become our parents. Parenting is a much bigger responsibility. Giving birth is appreciated but parenting is the continuous effort for a lifetime. While growing up in life, we become human and that's why some people remain animals till death. The better we think the more human we become. Think less and act better is always the best I listen everyday but don't overlook the power of right thinking. Thinking in the right direction is always the boon for humans.

Apply that animal theory in your life. Learn from animals how happy they are with what they have. Animals aren't bad. Our behaviour with them makes us bad. ***Remember first we also evolved from animals.***

CHAPTER SIXTEEN

2 I's of life: Imperfect Instance of Success

Curiosity brings two attributes in life, first is ideas & second is better imagination. We should apply these two I's in our life to think best when we have passion in our life. Everything is around us if we properly opened our vision instead of our eyes first. Some people find hard to think and imagine. Imagination is the only way to think from the other side where we can create a different world we always want to. If we can imagine, we can create too. *Imagination fulfils the law of attraction.* Ideas are in our imagination and vice versa. Most of the popular and successful entrepreneurs think after their imagination.

If we find everything boring, ideas don't get born in our minds. We have to be curious to think & imagine how life is working. How the world is working so smoothly. Theories and models are written after the practical aspects that come from the ideas in our life. No businessman was born with ideas; it's the curiosity to imagine a world where our imagination and ideas have also a particular space. Make your space and rethink what you actually want.

CHAPTER SEVENTEEN

Alpha, Beta, Gama (α β γ) Theory

Resolutions and oaths are significant to every year but how many resolutions remain unachieved, become bulk and leads to accumulated stress & less productivity in our life. When we plan we should accomplish it as soon as possible. Everyone has the habit of thinking about unaccomplished tasks and create unhappiness and stress. Plan little but accomplish it better. **Alpha, Beta and Gama theory says the simple way to achieve tasks which are given below:**

Alphaα- plan little, quick and better.

Beta β- Implement the same as soon as possible.

Gama γ- Don't make new plans until achieving αβfor the first stage.

As a writer, I am always surrounded by the ideas & sometimes get confused about whether to accomplish the current idea story or to move or get attracted to another fascinating idea. It happens with all of us. **Better we should apply our whole productivity of both in one idea.**We are flooded with the ideas but with less implementation in life. **Plan little and implement better to make Beta 2020 a new platform for other coming New Year's.**

Epilogue

I hate epilogue when it comes to writing for a self-help book but the conclusion is always significant when we do a particular task. I wrote what I find necessary to make it precise and useful. Make chapters notes to apply these principles in your life. Likewise, how I'm doing, you should conclude tasks so that we avoid unending, unnecessary thoughts and negative vibes in our minds. ***Beta 2020 can help us to enhance our personality, make us cheerful and a rising star. Believe yourself first then expect it from others.***

Choose happiness over the wrong people.

Choose peace over war.

Choose the right people for yourself.

Choose the sky than to look for an umbrella.

Ready for the worst but prepare for the best.

About The Author

Deepak Gupta is an enthralling Indian author with the great art of gripping storytelling. He is the ***#1 Bestselling***

Author of "She" and The Power of Nothing. He was born in Delhi, India. He graduated in commerce from Ramjas College, Delhi University and pursuing his Masters in commerce from Delhi school of economics. Recently his three books including *10 Principles to Beat Failure, The Lost Child and Earth 2200* were selected under ***Google Best Choice Award 2018.*** His ardency for inditing is authentically incontrovertible and unmatchable. He believes in inditing best exceptional content from his subconscious mind. He loves to observe, absorb and write on various social issues, inspirational truthful words, short stories and heart whelming poetry. He has travelled to many places in India like Manali, Rajasthan, Goa, Kolkata, Madhya Pradesh,   Jammu, Dalhousie and Mussoorie to bring descent originality in his work. He ***releases new short books every month***to get readers to connect with the truth of life. He lives in Delhi with his parents. You can electronically ***mail him at guptadeepak3111994@gmail.com***and follow him on ***twitter@authordeepakgup***and ***Instagram @authordeepakgupta***or like his official Facebook fan page ***(https://www.facebook.com/authordeepakgupta/).***

You can visit his official website: <u>**www.authordeepakgupta.com**</u>

Printed by Libri Plureos GmbH in Hamburg, Germany